salsas
dips and relishes

RYLAND
PETERS
& SMALL

LONDON NEW YORK

salsas
dips and relishes

Elsa Petersen-Schepelern
photography by Peter Cassidy

First published in the United States in 2002
by Ryland Peters & Small, Inc.
519 Broadway, 5th Floor
New York, NY 10012
www.rylandpeters.com

10 9 8 7 6 5 4 3 2

Text © Elsa Petersen-Schepelern 2002
Design and photographs
© Ryland Peters & Small 2002

Printed and bound in China

Library of Congress Cataloging-in-Publication Data

Petersen-Schepelern, Elsa.
   Salsas, dips, and relishes / Elsa Petersen-
   Schepelern ; photography by Peter Cassidy.
      p. cm.
   ISBN 1-84172-253-7
   1. Salsas (Cookery) 2. Dips (Appetizers)
   3. Cookery (Relishes) I. Title.

TX819.S29 P48 2002
641.8'14--dc21   2001048717

Notes

All spoon measurements are level.
Preheat ovens to the specified temperature. Recipes in this book were tested
with a regular oven. If using a convection oven, increase the cooking times
according to the manufacturer's instructions.
Uncooked or partly cooked eggs should not be served to the very young, the
very old or frail, or to pregnant women.

Senior Designer Steve Painter
Editor Siobhan O'Connor
Production Meryl Silbert
Art Director Gabriella Le Grazie
Publishing Director Alison Starling

Food Stylist Kate Habershon
Stylist Liz Belton

Author's acknowledgments

My thanks to my sister Kirsten and nephews Peter Bray and Luc Votan,
whose advice on this and every book is always much appreciated. Thanks
also to Sheridan Lear, the "Preserving Princess," and mates and fellow food
writers Clare Ferguson and Alastair Hendy, this time for their help with Salsa
Verde. My thanks also go to the endlessly good-humoured Kate Habershon, for
her beautiful food styling, and to her assistant Becka Heatherston. Appreciation, as
always, to photographer Peter Cassidy who just takes my breath away, to stylist Liz Belton,
and to Steve Painter for his wonderful design, again as usual. Thanks also to Pun Kum Thai
Restaurant in Whitfield Street, London W1, who lent their authentic Thai condiment set on page 31.

contents

Salsa isn't just a dance—it's also a salad's groovy cousin or a sauce with extra pizzazz. Though we think of it as Mexican or Latin American, other countries also have their own versions. This book includes salsas, sauces, and other dips from around the world—plus the sorts of quick pickles and relishes that don't require a preserving pan. Most can be made only a few minutes or an hour in advance—just enough time to develop savor and piquancy. The best thing is—they're healthy and delicious.

not just a dance ...

Avocado is a Mexican ingredient, so it tastes good in a salsa (which is, after all, a Latin American dish). Many people cut avocado into dice, but I like it scooped out with a teaspoon, all rough and creamy. Whatever you do, don't bother with any avocado except the warty-skinned, greenish-purple Hass. I grew up in an avocado-growing area and I can tell you that other varieties aren't worth the trouble.

avocado chile salsa
with chargrilled shrimp

2 red onions, quartered, then finely sliced

1 red chile, such as serrano, seeded and sliced or diced

finely grated zest and juice of 1 lime

2 large, ripe Hass avocados, halved, with pits removed*

2 ripe red tomatoes, halved, seeded, and diced

a large handful of cilantro

salt and coarsely cracked black pepper

Chargrilled shrimp

3–5 uncooked shrimp per person, depending on size, with shells

2 tablespoons chile oil

juice of 2 limes

a pinch of salt

2 tablespoons brown sugar

Serves 4

To make the salsa, put the onion, chile, and half the lime juice into a bowl and set aside to marinate for a few minutes.

Using a small teaspoon or coffee spoon, scoop out small balls of avocado into a serving bowl. Add the lime zest and remaining juice and turn gently to coat. This will stop the avocado turning brown.

Add the diced tomatoes to the onion mixture, toss gently, then add the avocado. Tear the cilantro over the top and sprinkle with the salt and black pepper. Serve the salsa with the chargrilled shrimp, or with meat or chicken marinated in a chile-olive oil marinade, then chargrilled. Warmed flour tortillas, sour cream, and lettuce are also delicious accompaniments.

Chargrilled shrimp Slit the shrimp down the back and pull out the black vein, if any. Put the chile oil, lime juice, salt, and sugar into a bowl, add the shrimp, and toss to coat. Using your fingers, push the sauce into the slit and set aside for 30 minutes. Preheat a stove-top grill pan or outdoor grill to medium hot, add the shrimp, then cook on both sides until just opaque. Serve with the avocado chile salsa.

*Note Always prepare avocado at the last moment and coat in a little citrus juice. Avocado turns brown very quickly—don't believe the old wives' tale that the pit prevents this.

salsas

2 ears of corn, husks removed,
brushed with corn oil

2 red bell peppers,
quartered and seeded

2 long red chiles, such as New
Mexico, halved and seeded

4 ripe tomatoes, halved,
seeded, and finely diced

1 red onion, chopped

2 garlic cloves, crushed

2 tablespoons chopped
or torn cilantro

salt and freshly ground black
pepper (optional)

Dressing

½ teaspoon sugar

1 tablespoon corn oil

juice of 1 lime

1 teaspoon salt, or to taste

freshly cracked black pepper

Barbecue spareribs

2 garlic cloves, crushed

2 tablespoons salt

2 tablespoons ground cumin

1 teaspoon Tabasco sauce

1 teaspoon dried oregano

½ cup honey

¼ cup sherry vinegar

⅓ cup olive oil

2 lb. barbecue spareribs

Serves 4

The Mexican habit of grilling salsa ingredients first gives them a delicious, smoky, barbecue flavor. Toasted chiles, corn, peppers, and even tomatoes all benefit from a bit of fire!

chile corn salsa
with barbecue spareribs

Put the corn, pepper quarters, and chile halves onto a preheated outdoor grill or under the broiler. Toast until the pepper and chile skins and the corn are all lightly charred. Cool, then pull off the pepper and chile skins (leaving a few charred bits behind) and slice the kernels off the corn cob. Put into a bowl, add the tomatoes, onion, and garlic, then toss well.

To make the dressing, put the sugar, corn oil, lime juice, salt, and pepper into a bowl or pitcher, mix well, then pour over the vegetables and toss again. Cover and chill for at least 30 minutes. Before serving, stir through the chopped or torn cilantro. Taste and add extra salt and freshly cracked black pepper if necessary.

Barbecue spareribs To make a marinade, put the garlic, salt, cumin, Tabasco, oregano, honey, vinegar, and olive oil into a shallow dish and mix. Pat the ribs dry with paper towels, add them to the dish, then rub in the marinade. Cover and chill overnight.

When ready to cook, preheat an outdoor grill to medium, then add the ribs, and cook on both sides for about 30 minutes until done. Baste from time to time with the marinade.

Cut the ribs into slices, each side of the bones, and arrange on 4 serving plates. Serve with the salsa beside or in a separate bowl. Have lots of napkins for mopping up, plus lots of cold beer.

Some people like the skin on peppers—personally, I find it indigestible and the easiest way to remove it is with a vegetable peeler. Green bell peppers are just unripe ordinary peppers—if you prefer ripe ones, use other colors. I love Chinese yard-long beans in salads, because they keep their crunch, but use regular beans if these are difficult to find.

green apple salsa

3 green bell peppers

2 Chinese yard-long beans, cut in 4, or 10 green beans

8 inches cucumber

a large handful of scallions or 1 white onion

juice of 1½–2 oranges

2 Granny Smith apples, cored and diced

a large bunch of mint or basil, about 4 oz., finely chopped (optional)

salt and freshly ground black pepper

Serves 4

Using a vegetable peeler, peel the peppers. Cut off the stalks and seed. Cut into strips lengthwise, then into dice, about ¼ inch.

Top and tail the beans, then steam or microwave until cooked but still crisp. Plunge immediately into cold water and run the cold water until the beans are quite cool. Pat dry and cut into dice.

Cut the cucumber in half lengthwise and scrape out the seed section. This is very sour and liquid, so I like it removed, but this is optional. Cut the cucumber into strips, then into dice.

Cut the scallions into short dice or, if using white a onion, cut into ¼-inch dice.

Put the peppers, beans, cucumber, and scallions or onion into a bowl, squeeze over the orange juice, then sprinkle with salt and pepper. Set aside for at least 30 minutes to develop the flavor. Just before serving, add the diced apple and toss to coat with the juice.

Serve as is, or shred the mint or basil, sprinkle over the top, then serve. This salsa is an excellent accompaniment for duck, chargrilled pork chops, or chunks of boiled ham.

Sweet fruits, hot chiles, and scented herbs make a great salsa combination. Papaya is wonderful because it's rich and creamy, but mango, pineapple, and other tropical fruits such as lychees would also be delicious.

papaya chile salsa
with chargrilled tuna

1 fresh ripe papaya

1 red bell pepper

1 yellow bell pepper

1 red chile, such as serrano, seeded and chopped

1 tablespoon grated fresh ginger

a large handful of cilantro, torn

finely grated zest and juice of 3 limes

salt and freshly ground black pepper

Chargrilled tuna

4 small tuna steaks or 2 large

2 tablespoons peanut oil

1 tablespoon lemon juice

1 red chile, finely chopped

lime wedges, to serve

Serves 4

To prepare the tuna, put it into a bowl and sprinkle with the oil, lemon juice, and chile. Toss to coat and let marinate while you prepare and marinate the salsa.

To make the salsa, peel the papaya and peppers with a vegetable peeler. Cut them in half and remove the seeds. Chop into ½-inch dice. Put into a bowl, then add the chile and ginger. Stir in the cilantro, lime zest and juice, salt, and pepper. Set aside for 30 minutes before serving.

When ready to cook, pat the tuna dry with paper towels. Preheat a stove-top grill pan, then cook very quickly on both sides until barred with brown stripes, but still pink in the middle. Don't overcook the tuna or it will be dry and tasteless.

Serve on heated dinner plates with the salsa and wedges of lime.

Breathtakingly simple, but wonderful in taste, serve this salsa as an accompaniment for meat, fish, or poultry, on pizza, or crushed onto bruschetta. Best of all is with these sweet little lamb cutlets. I like to spoon the salsa into a small bowl on the plate, with the cutlets beside. This is great food for an outdoor party—the cutlets can be eaten with the fingers and the salsa with a teaspoon.

roasted tomato and oregano salsa
with lamb cutlets

12 plum tomatoes, about 1½-inches diameter

4 sprigs of oregano

⅓ cup extra virgin olive oil

2 garlic cloves, finely sliced

2 tablespoons balsamic vinegar

a pinch of salt flakes, crushed

1 teaspoon harissa paste or a dash of Tabasco sauce

brown sugar (optional)

1 tablespoon freshly cracked black peppercorns

Lamb cutlets

12 lamb cutlets (from a rack of lamb), frenched and chined, then all fat removed

olive oil, for sautéing

salt and freshly ground black pepper

a few oregano leaves, to serve

Serves 4

Prick the tomatoes once each with a toothpick. Put the tomatoes and oregano into a plastic bag with 2 tablespoons of the olive oil and the garlic. Shake to coat with oil, then transfer to a roasting pan and roast in a preheated oven at 400°F until half collapsed, with the tomato skins split and slightly browned, about 15–30 minutes, depending on the size of the tomatoes. Brown under the broiler if necessary.

To make the dressing, put the balsamic vinegar into a bowl, add the remaining olive oil, the salt and harissa or Tabasco, and beat with a fork. Add brown sugar to taste, if using, and stir to dissolve. Put the tomatoes into small serving bowls, pour over the dressing, and sprinkle with pepper. Keep them warm in the turned-off oven while you sauté the cutlets.

To cook the cutlets, put the oil into a skillet, heat well, then add the cutlets, in batches if necessary, and sprinkle with salt. Sauté at a high heat for about 1–2 minutes on each side until browned but still pink in the middle. Divide the cutlets between 4 heated dinner plates and add the small bowls of tomatoes. Sprinkle with oregano, salt, and cracked black pepper. Serve with small spoons to eat the tomatoes.

Note Roast the tomatoes on the vines if you prefer. Some people think tomatoes on the vine have more flavor—I think they just cost more.

Thai pesto is usually used as a topping for the fish before it's cooked, but I prefer the fresh, bright tastes when it's uncooked. The solution— serve it as a salsa accompaniment. Salmon isn't an Asian fish, but its creamy richness goes very well with the sweet, spicy, scented flavors of Southeast Asia.

thai pesto with fish fillets

1 cup mint or Asian basil (not regular basil), torn

2 stalks of lemongrass, finely sliced

2 garlic cloves, crushed

2 teaspoons fish sauce

1 tablespoon freshly squeezed lime juice

¼ cup peanut or canola oil

1 tablespoon Thai sweet chile sauce

4 oz. cilantro, torn, about 3 cups

To serve

4–8 fish fillets, such as salmon

peanut oil, for cooking

salad leaves, to serve

Serves 4

To make the pesto, put the mint or basil, lemongrass, garlic, fish sauce, and lime juice into a blender or food processor and blend until coarsely chopped. With the motor running, add the peanut oil and chile sauce. (Alternatively, use a mortar and pestle.) Scoop into a bowl and stir in the torn cilantro.

Brush the salmon with the oil. Heat a stove-top grill pan until hot, add the fish skin side down, and cook for about 2–3 minutes or until the fish can easily be moved in the pan. Turn it over and cook the other side for about 1 minute—the fish should still be pink in the middle. Top with the pesto and serve with salad.

three raitas with naan

Raita is the Indian version of a salsa, mixed with yogurt dressing. Serve with chunks of naan bread or with fiery curries—yogurt and other dairy foods are able to cool the fires of chile burns because the chemicals in chiles are fat-soluble, not water-soluble. Drinking water or beer won't cool the burn, but yogurt will. It's a particularly healthful ingredient—and can be low-fat, too, if you like.

The first recipe, using yogurt and mint, is a common combination, but in India, of course, they can't resist adding chiles. I like just a little—but please yourself (and your guests!)

The second combination of onion, tomato, chiles, and cucumber makes a great salsa by itself, but when bathed in yogurt, it's creamy and delicious and the sauce turns a pretty blush pink.

The third is made with cucumber: cucumber and yogurt make one of the classic flavor combinations—a popular cooling food, especially as an accompaniment to chile dishes.

chile and mint

leaves from a large bunch of mint

1 teaspoon salt

½ teaspoon sugar

1 cup plain yogurt

1 green chile, finely sliced

Makes about 2 cups

Put the mint into a blender and blend until finely chopped. Add the salt, sugar, and yogurt, and blend briefly. Transfer to a bowl and serve, sprinkled with the sliced green chile.

tomato, onion, and chile

1 cup yogurt

1 teaspoon salt

1 teaspoon sugar

juice of ½ lemon

1 red onion, finely diced

1 tomato, seeded and chopped

2 inches cucumber, halved, seeded, and chopped*

1 fresh red chile, chopped

1 fresh green chile, chopped

Makes about 2 cups

Put the yogurt, salt, sugar, and lemon juice into a bowl and mix to dissolve the sugar. Add the onion, tomato, and chiles, stir gently, chill for 30 minutes, then serve.

cucumber and ginger

1 cup yogurt

1 inch fresh ginger, peeled and grated

1 teaspoon salt

1 tablespoon sugar

1 tablespoon lemon juice

½ teaspoon ground turmeric

2 inches cucumber*

Makes about 2 cups

Put the yogurt, ginger, salt, sugar, lemon juice, and turmeric into a bowl and mix to dissolve the sugar.

Cut the ends off the cucumber, cut in half lengthwise, and scrape out the seeds with a teaspoon. If the skin is tough or waxed, peel it off: otherwise, leave it on. Cut the cucumber into matchstick strips, put into a bowl, and pour over the yogurt dressing. Chill for about 30 minutes, then serve.

*Note If you have time, sprinkle the prepared, seeded cucumber with salt and set aside to drain for at least 10 minutes. Rinse and pat dry with paper towels before using. This will remove some of the bitter juices which would otherwise seep into the dressing.

12 dried New Mexico chiles

¼ cup peanut or canola oil

3 garlic cloves

1 tablespoon chopped fresh oregano

6 large, ripe tomatoes, peeled and seeded

salt

corn chips, to serve

Makes about 2 cups

Break the chiles in half and remove the seeds. Heat the oil in a skillet, add the chiles, and sauté until they turn bright red. Remove with a slotted spoon and put into a bowl. Cover with water and let soak for about 30 minutes, then drain.

Add the garlic to the skillet and sauté until golden. Transfer to a food processor, add the drained chiles, oregano, and tomatoes and chop coarsely. Add salt and pepper to taste and serve with corn chips. Alternatively, serve as an all-purpose sauce for the table—add it to any dish.

salsa roja with corn chips

Mexican salsas aren't just chopped fresh salads. Mexico, too, has the "sauce" kind of salsa—versions of this one can be found on restaurant and diner tables all over the country. Add it to anything you think needs a bit of livening up, or serve with corn chips and lots of Margaritas.

salsa verde
with soft-cooked eggs and baby leeks

3 tablespoons capers in salt

2 cups fresh parsley leaves

2 garlic cloves, crushed

3 anchovy fillets

⅓ cup olive oil

½ tablespoon sherry vinegar

To serve

8 oz. baby leeks

6 small eggs

salt and freshly ground black pepper

Serves 6

I find many salsa verde recipes too violently sour, but this one is smooth and delicious, and goes with any mild-tasting foods. Friend and fellow food writer, Alastair Hendy, serves it with leeks: it's also good with eggs and with poached chicken breasts.

To make the salsa verde, put the capers into a bowl, add water, and let soak to remove the salt, about 10–15 minutes, changing the water at least once. Pour off the water and remove the capers, leaving the salt behind.

Put the parsley into a small food processor and chop coarsely. Add the capers, garlic, and anchovies, and chop again. Pour in about 3–4 tablespoons of the olive oil and the vinegar, blend again, and taste. Add the remaining olive oil if preferred—the sauce should be thick and paste-like, not liquid.

Meanwhile, cut the leeks down two-thirds of their length, leaving them attached at the root end. Cut again into quarters and wash thoroughly to remove all grit and sand. Transfer to a steamer and steam until tender, about 5–10 minutes (the time depends on the size of the leeks).

Put the eggs into a small saucepan of cold water and bring to a boil: from the point of boiling, time them for 4 minutes. Drain and run under cold water to stop them cooking further. Drain again and tap all over to crack the shells. Gently peel off the shells (carefully, because the eggs will be soft). Carefully cut them in half lengthwise and put onto a serving platter. Drain the leeks and add them to the platter. Serve the salsa verde spooned over the leeks, or transfer to a separate bowl.

tabbouleh in party pitas

1 cup medium bulghur

a very large bunch of
flat-leaf parsley

a very large bunch of mint

2 large, ripe tomatoes,
halved and seeded

3 scallions, sliced

2 tablespoons extra virgin olive oil

1 tablespoon freshly squeezed
lemon juice

salt and cracked black pepper

Chile sauce

1 teaspoon harissa paste
or 2 dashes Tabasco sauce

¼ cup olive oil

salt

Party pitas

20 mini pita breads

1 quantity of hummus (page 43)

½ cup plain yogurt

6-inch squares of wax paper,
folded into cones

Serves 20 as party food or
4 as an accompaniment

Tabbouleh is a great Lebanese classic salad—it should be green, with tons of parsley and mint (there should be so much green that you hardly notice the bulghur or tomatoes). Here, it's served as party food in mini pita breads with a dollop of hummus and homemade chile sauce in a separate bowl for people to help themselves. It's also great with kabobs and felafel.

To make the tabbouleh, soak the bulghur in water for 20 minutes, then drain. Coarsely chop the parsley and mint.

Put the tomatoes, chopped herbs, scallions, and bulghur into a bowl. Sprinkle with the oil and lemon juice, add salt and pepper to taste, and toss well.

To make the chile sauce, put the harissa paste or Tabasco into a dipping bowl, add the olive oil, and stir well. Add salt to taste.

Party pitas Heat the pitas in a microwave or in the oven according to the package instructions. Cut in half. Add a teaspoon of hummus to each half pocket and another teaspoon of plain yogurt. Top with the tabbouleh and serve wrapped in little wax paper cones with the dipping bowl of chile sauce for people to help themselves.

red pesto

Ordinary green pesto can be expensive to make unless you grow your own basil or have a farmer's market nearby where you can buy it by the armful, rather than in cute little packages from the supermarket. Red pesto, on the other hand, is easy to make, as long as you have sun-dried tomatoes in the pantry. This recipe is a thousand times better than the store-bought version. Serve it in the usual way, as a sauce stirred through pasta, cooked on top of pizza, on mini toasts as party food, or as a flavor-enhancer in meat or poultry sauces.

3 oz. sun-dried tomatoes

½ cup pine nuts

¼ cup freshly grated Parmesan cheese

½ cup olive oil

Makes about 1½ cups

Put the sun-dried tomatoes into a bowl, cover with 1 cup boiling water and let soak overnight. Drain, reserving the liquid for another use (such as adding flavor to soups and stews). Chop the tomatoes with kitchen shears.

Put the pine nuts into a dry skillet and heat gently until golden. Take care—they burn easily. Remove from the pan and let cool.

Put the toasted pine nuts into a blender and work to a meal. Add the drained tomatoes and Parmesan and blend again. Slowly drizzle in the olive oil to form a thick paste.

palm sugar

1 cylinder palm sugar or
2 tablespoons brown sugar

If using palm sugar
(available from Asian
stores), put it on a board
and shave off shards with
a knife—enough to half-fill
a small bowl.

red chile flakes

a large handful of large
red dried chiles

Put the chiles into a dry
skillet and heat gently
until aromatic. Take care,
because they burn easily.

Using a small blender
or mortar and pestle,
crush into flakes. To
be authentic, keep the
seeds in the mixture,
but, if you prefer, you
can remove as many as
possible before crushing.
Serve the flakes in a
small bowl.

chile fish sauce

3 fresh red bird's eye chiles,
finely sliced crosswise

½ cup fish sauce

Put the sliced chiles and
fish sauce into a bowl,
stir briefly, then transfer
to a small bowl.

chile vinegar sauce

½ cup white rice vinegar

3 fresh green bird's eye
chiles, finely sliced
crosswise

Put the vinegar and
chiles into a small jar,
shake to mix, then set
aside. When ready to
serve, transfer to a
small bowl.

thai condiments

Southeast Asian homes and restaurants don't usually keep salt and pepper on the
table. Instead, they have a "cruet" of condiments, such as this one from Thailand.
They include toasted dried red chile flakes, sugar—usually palm sugar—and chiles
steeped in fish sauce and vinegar, plus a separate bowl of chopped peanuts. Serve
these condiments as great accompaniments for many Thai dishes, including noodles.

dips and **relishes**

vietnamese spring rolls
with pickles and dipping sauce

3 oz. beanthread noodles (2 bundles)

1 package Vietnamese ricepaper wrappers (*bahn trang*)

1 butterhead lettuce, leaves finely shredded

a large bunch of Vietnamese herbs, such as cilantro and mint

Chinese barbecued pork, duck, or shrimp*

Pickled carrots and radishes

1–2 carrots

about 10 radishes

2 teaspoons rice vinegar

2 pinches of salt

4 teaspoons sugar

Nuòc cham dipping sauce

1 garlic clove, crushed

½ small, hot red chile, such as bird's eye, finely chopped

1 tablespoon sugar

juice from 1 wedge of lime

2 tablespoons fish sauce

Serves 4

Vietnam has produced one of the world's truly great cuisines— fresh with salads and herbs, and less oily than Chinese. This recipe includes several of its greatest components; fresh pickles and a sublime dipping sauce.

To make the pickles, peel the carrots, and cut into long, thin strips with a vegetable peeler. Roll up and cut into thin strips. Alternatively, slice on a mandoline. Finely slice the radishes on a mandoline—aim for see-through slices. Put the carrots into one bowl and the radishes into another. Divide the vinegar, salt, and sugar between the bowls, then add ½ cup water to each one. Set aside for at least 15 minutes or up to 24 hours. Drain before using.

To make the dipping sauce, grind the garlic, chile, and sugar to a paste with a mortar and pestle. Add the lime juice, fish sauce, and 2½ tablespoons water.

Soak the beanthread noodles in hot water for 15 minutes, then drain, and keep in cold water until ready to serve.

To prepare the spring rolls, dip 1 ricepaper sheet in a dish of water for about 30 seconds until softened. Put onto a plate (not a board, or they will dry out). On one side of the sheet, put a few shreds of lettuce, noodles, herbs, pork, duck, or shrimp, and pickled carrot and radish. There should be lots of herbs.

Roll up the ricepaper like a cigar and repeat until all the ingredients have been used. Put the rolls on a serving platter, spray with a mist of water, and cover with a damp cloth or paper towel until ready to serve. To serve, spray with water again and serve with the dipping sauce. Alternatively, serve the ingredients on separate plates for guests to assemble their own rolls.

*Note If unavailable, rub 2 duck breasts with Chinese five-spice powder and let marinate for 15 minutes. Transfer to a preheated skillet, skin side down, and cook for about 10 minutes until the skin is crisp, the fat runs, and the flesh is cooked half through. Turn them over and cook the other side until medium rare. Set aside, let cool, then shred or slice finely.

chinese spiced salt

1 tablespoon Szechuan peppercorns

1 tablespoon red peppercorns

1 tablespoon white peppercorns

1 tablespoon green peppercorns

1 tablespoon black peppercorns

¼ cup salt flakes

Makes about ½ cup

Put the peppercorns into a dry skillet and heat gently to release the aromas. Transfer to a blender or mortar and pestle, add the salt, and blend briefly until coarsely crushed. Transfer to a small dipping bowl and serve.

*Note To make fries, cut them to your preferred size, soak in ice water for 20 minutes, rinse, and pat dry with paper towels. Sauté first at 350°F until pale gold, then drain, increase the heat to 385°F and sauté for a few minutes more or until golden brown. Drain on paper towels, sprinkle with salt, then serve.

chubby fries with ...

The classic accompaniments for French fries* are salt, pepper, and ketchup. These three fiery dips are spicy variations and are also terrific with other dishes, such as rare roast beef, chargrilled shrimp, or party foods of many kinds. Cook skinny fries if you like, but I like mine of a more substantial nature.

wasabi mayonnaise

2 egg yolks

1 extra whole egg (if using a blender)

2 tablespoons lemon juice

½ teaspoon Dijon mustard

a pinch of salt

1 cup cold-pressed oil, such as peanut (not olive)

3–4 tablespoons wasabi paste (1 tube)

Makes about 2 cups

Put the egg yolks and whole egg into a blender, add the lemon juice, mustard, a pinch of salt, and ¼ cup of the oil. Turn on the machine and blend until creamy, a few seconds. Add the remaining oil, a tablespoon at a time, drizzling in slowly. Add in stages, not in a thin stream as most books advise.

When all the oil has been added, if the mixture is too thick, add a teaspoon or so of warm water.

Stir in the wasabi paste just before serving.

chile lemongrass vinegar

2 cups white rice vinegar or cider vinegar

4 stalks of lemongrass, trimmed and sliced lengthwise

2 fresh red chiles, such as serrano, sliced lengthwise and seeded

1 bottle, 2 cups, sterilized

Makes 2 cups

Put the vinegar into a stainless steel saucepan and warm gently. Put the lemongrass and chiles into the prepared bottle. Using a funnel, fill the bottle with the warmed vinegar. Let cool before sealing with a cork.

Keep the bottle on the windowsill for 7–14 days, then use immediately or strain into a clean, sterilized bottle.

Make this tapenade with green or black olives—the best quality you can find. Use it (and the marmalade on the next page) as a topping for thinly sliced, toasted baguettes or black bread and serve with drinks before dinner.

toasted baguettes with **tapenade**

1½ cups green or black olives, such as niçoise, pitted

1 tablespoon capers in salt, or caperberries, rinsed and patted dry

3 anchovy fillets, rinsed and chopped

1 tablespoon freshly squeezed lemon juice

1½ tablespoons extra virgin olive oil

sliced baguette, bruschetta or Melba toast, to serve

Makes about 1 cup

Using a mortar and pestle, grind the pitted olives, capers or caperberries, and anchovies into a paste. Add the olive oil in a thin stream, then add the lemon juice. Alternatively, use a small blender.

Serve with thin slices of baguette, or on bruschetta or Melba toast.

¼ cup olive oil

2 lb. red onions, finely sliced

1 bay leaf

2 chiles, such as serrano, seeded
and finely sliced (optional)

1 tablespoon sugar

1 tablespoon red wine vinegar

a pinch of salt

1 tablespoon crème de cassis

a pinch of ground allspice

small pieces of toast, to serve

Makes about 1 cup

red onion marmalade

Heat the oil in a heavy skillet, add the onions, bay
leaf, chiles, if using, and sugar, and stir-fry until the
onions start to soften. Cover with a lid and let steam
for about 15 minutes so the onions will soften.

Remove the lid and continue cooking over low heat for
about 30 minutes until almost melted. Add the vinegar,
salt, crème de cassis, and allspice.

Continue cooking gently until the onions have become
thick and jam-like. Remove from the heat, let cool,
then keep in a lidded container in the refrigerator until
ready to use. Serve on small toasts with drinks.

You can make this marmalade with ordinary onions, but red onions, red wine
vinegar, and crème de cassis will make for a rosy result. Use the rest of the
bottle of crème de cassis to make Kir Royales to serve with the toasts.

baba ganoush

Baba ganoush is the famous creamy eggplant purée with smoky overtones. It's best to char them over an open fire or outdoor grill to achieve the authentic smoky flavor, but, if you don't have one, a hot broiler or the open flame on a gas stove are also fine. Serve baba ganoush as a dip for parties or with other dishes as an appetizer.

3 eggplant

¼ cup plain yogurt

2 tablespoons tahini paste

1 garlic clove, crushed

1 teaspoon salt

juice of 1–2 lemons, to taste

1 tablespoon chopped fresh flat-leaf parsley (optional)

pita breads, warmed or lightly toasted, to serve

Serves 8

Put the eggplant on top of the open gas flame on top of the stove and cook until well charred on all sides. The steam created inside the vegetable will cook the flesh. The eggplant must be charred all over and soft in the middle. Remove from the flame and let cool on a plate.

When cool, carefully pull off the skins and stems. Don't leave any charred bits. Put the flesh into a bowl, then blend with a hand-held stick blender or fork: the texture should not be too smooth. Add the yogurt, tahini, garlic, and salt, and blend again.

Add the juice of 1 lemon, taste, then gradually add more juice until you achieve flavor and texture to your taste. Transfer to a serving bowl and sprinkle with finely chopped parsley, if using.

Serve with wedges of toasted pita breads for scooping the dip.

hummus
with flat beans

I serve this unusual combination with drinks before dinner. People are always surprised, but then have to be prevented from overdosing on it, in order to leave room for the rest of the meal.

1 cup dried chickpeas

1 teaspoon salt

⅓ cup tahini paste

freshly squeezed juice of 1–2 lemons, or to taste

2 garlic cloves, crushed

salt, to taste

To serve

1 tablespoon olive oil

1 teaspoon harissa paste or paprika

8 oz. uncooked flat beans or runner beans, sliced diagonally into 2-inch pieces

Serves 6

Put the chickpeas into a saucepan and cover with 3 cups boiling water. Soak for 12 hours or overnight.

When ready to cook, drain the chickpeas, transfer to a saucepan, cover with fresh water, and bring to a boil. Reduce the heat and simmer gently until almost tender (the time will depend on the age of the beans and where they were grown). When almost done, add 1 teaspoon salt, and simmer until soft. Drain, reserving a little of the cooking water. (Do not add salt at the beginning of cooking or the beans will stay tough.)

Drain the beans and transfer to a blender. Purée until smooth, then press through a strainer or food mill to remove the remains of the tough skins.

Stir in the tahini paste and the juice of 1 lemon, then the crushed garlic. Taste and add salt or extra lemon juice to taste, and a little of the cooking water, until you achieve a creamy purée.

Spoon into a bowl and make a swirl with a teaspoon. Put the olive oil and harissa or paprika into a cup, stir well, then pour the mixture into the swirls. Put the bowl on a serving dish, add the flat beans or runner beans, then serve.

stir-fried okra salsa
with mustard seed relish

½ cup peanut or canola oil

1 tablespoon mustard seeds

2 red onions, diced or sliced

3 garlic cloves, crushed

2 tablespoons grated fresh ginger

about 1 lb. fresh okra, trimmed and cut crosswise into ½-inch chunks

salt and freshly ground black pepper

1–2 small, mild green chiles, sliced (optional)

Onion and mustard seed relish

¼ cup peanut or canola oil

1 tablespoon mustard seeds

1 cup grated onion

1 inch fresh ginger, grated

4 garlic cloves, crushed

½–1 teaspoon ground turmeric

a pinch of salt, or to taste

Serves 4

This mustard seed relish is a variation on a traditional Indian technique called "tempering." The relish is added to many dishes as a last-minute flavor-enhancer. When served separately, it's great as a topping for grilled meat and poultry. The cooked salsa is also based on an Indian vegetarian dish, and Indian cooks have solved the age-old dilemma of how to stop okra juices turning to ooze. The secret is never to let a single drop of water touch them at any stage of cooking. Before cooking okra, wash and pat very dry with paper towels, then let dry completely before cutting. If you never liked okra before, I think you'll find this dish the exception.

To make the salsa, put the oil into a skillet over medium heat, then add the mustard seeds. Stir-fry until they pop. Add the onion, garlic, and ginger with salt and pepper to taste. Stir-fry until softened and translucent. Add the okra and stir-fry until cooked but crisp, then stir in the chiles, if using.

To make the onion and mustard seed relish, put the oil into a skillet over moderate heat. When hot, add the mustard seeds. Sauté until they pop, then stir in the onion, ginger, garlic, turmeric, and salt. Cook until the onion softens and browns slightly.

Serve the okra with the relish in a separate small bowl, for guests to help themselves.

6 long peppers or 8 bell, red, yellow, and orange

2–3 medium-hot chiles

2 teaspoons salt

¼ cup extra virgin olive oil

2–4 tablespoons rice vinegar, sherry vinegar, or cider vinegar

To serve

a handful of oregano leaves

cracked black pepper

Serves 4–8, with other dishes

Cut the peppers and chiles in half lengthwise, leaving them attached at the stem end. Scrape out the membranes and seeds. Put the peppers and chiles under a preheated broiler and cook until the skins are charred. Remove to a stainless steel saucepan and cover with a lid. Let steam to loosen the skins. Remove the skins, retaining any juices in the saucepan.

Arrange the peppers and chiles in a plastic container with a lid. Add any juices from the saucepan and sprinkle with the salt, oil, and vinegar. Cover and set aside for 30 minutes or up to 2 days in the refrigerator.

To serve, top with the oregano and pepper, and serve with antipasti, pizza, or bruschetta.

pickled peppers

When grilled or broiled, peppers take on a marvelous sweet flavor—add a quick pickle of salt and vinegar and you have a deliciously bright taste. Leave out the chiles if you like your pickles cool. I prefer the smooth, mild flavor of rice vinegar, but sherry and cider vinegars are great, too. The longer you leave the mixture, the more "pickled" it will become.

quick **pickles**

Zucchini aren't always green. Yellow squash are very sweet in flavor (there is a green-and-white striped variety, too). I particularly like the baby ones, about 2–3 inches long (zucchini, an Italian word, means "little squash"), but have used slightly bigger ones for this dish.

zucchini and rosemary with pepper oil

3 green zucchini

3 yellow squash

salt

¼ cup extra virgin olive oil

a small handful of tiny sprigs of rosemary (the smallest end leaves), to serve

1–2 tablespoons peppercorns, red, black, and green, cracked

shredded zest of 1 lemon

2 tablespoons cider vinegar

Red pepper oil

4 red bell peppers

1 cup extra virgin olive oil

Serves 4–8

To make the red pepper oil, quarter and seed the peppers, put them on a shallow baking tray and broil, skin side up, until soft and the skins are blackened. Remove from the heat and transfer to a saucepan, adding any juices from the tray. Put on the lid and set aside for a few minutes to steam off the skins. Pull or scrape off the skins, reserving any juices.

Transfer the peppers, juices, and olive oil to a blender and purée until smooth. Let settle. Strain off the liquid into a bowl or pitcher.

Cut the zucchini and yellow squash into ¼-inch slices lengthwise. Put onto a plate and sprinkle with salt. Set aside to drain for about 30 minutes. Discard the liquid, rinse off the salt, and pat dry with paper towels.

Put the slices into a plastic bag, add the olive oil, and shake until coated. Transfer to a preheated stove-top grill pan and cook for about 3 minutes on one side, without moving them. The flesh should be barred with lines and just becoming translucent around the edges. Turn them over and cook the other side until lightly barred with brown. They should be tender, but not too soft.

Transfer to a long, shallow serving dish and sprinkle with the rosemary sprigs and cracked pepper. Sprinkle with the lemon zest and vinegar, and let marinate for 30 minutes or overnight. If leaving overnight, cover and chill. Return to room temperature to serve.

Sprinkle with the pepper oil and serve as antipasti, on bruschetta, or in baguettes with cheese.

These oven-dried tomatoes achieve some of the flavor of sun-dried without the leathery texture. The quick pickling effect of balsamic vinegar gives a rather sweet flavor—other vinegars such as sherry and cider give a lighter taste. Ordinary fresh sliced tomato is also great dressed simply with pepper and a sprinkle of vinegar—never mind the oil or the salt. Try it.

oven-dried tomatoes
with roasted garlic, balsamic, and thyme

24 small plum tomatoes or other small tomatoes

sugar

salt flakes, preferably sea salt

2–3 garlic cloves, cut into fine slivers

about 2 tablespoons balsamic vinegar, to sprinkle

1 tablespoon thyme leaves

Serves 4

Halve the tomatoes crosswise and cut out the dense central core with a sharp knife. Arrange apart on oven trays. On each half, put a small pinch of sugar and a few salt flakes. Push 2 small slivers of garlic into each half.

Roast in a preheated oven at 400°F for about 20 minutes, then reduce the heat to 300°F for another 10 minutes. When collapsed, soft, and starting to brown, remove from the oven*.

To make a quick pickle, sprinkle them with balsamic vinegar and thyme leaves and set aside to marinate for about 30 minutes. At this point, they can be used as a topping on pizzas and bruschetta, or served as a salsa.

*Note If you cook the tomatoes for 15–30 minutes more (or longer, depending on size) at the lowest temperature, they will dry out into an approximation of sun-dried tomatoes (only, I think, better). When dried, they are good served with cocktails.

You can use precooked beets for this dish, but, if you're cooking them yourself, make sure there aren't any cuts on the skins and don't cut off the stalk end or the thin root. If you do, all the beautiful color will seep out into the water. Use store-bought pâté, or my family recipe below.

danish spiced beets with pâté

2 lb. small cooked beets

1 tablespoon cloves

1 tablespoon allspice berries, coarsely crushed

3 cinnamon sticks, broken

1¼ cups white wine vinegar

about ½ cup sugar

Danish liver pâté

8 oz. chopped fatty bacon

1 lb. lamb's liver, trimmed and cut into 1-inch pieces

1 egg

1 teaspoon salt

2 teaspoons freshly ground black pepper

2 teaspoons ground allspice

2 anchovy fillets

1 tablespoon butter

1 tablespoon all-purpose flour

1 cup milk

2 large onions, finely chopped

Serves about 20

Cut off the tops and bottoms of the cooked beets and slip off the skins. Slice the beets finely—on a mandoline, if you have one—then pack the slices into preserving jars, putting the cloves, allspice, and cinnamon sticks between the layers.

Put the vinegar and sugar into a small saucepan, then bring to a boil, and simmer until the sugar has dissolved. Pour into the jars until the beets are completely covered—if the jars are large, you may have to prepare more vinegar and sugar mixture.

Seal the jars and use within 7 days. Serve with pâté on light rye bread, pumpernickel, toast, or brown bread.

Danish liver pâté Put the bacon into a food processor and work to a paste. Remove and set aside. Put the liver into the processor and blend until smooth. Add the bacon, then the egg, salt, pepper, allspice, and anchovies. Meanwhile, put the butter into a saucepan, heat until melted, then stir in the flour and cook for 1 minute. Gradually stir in the milk and cook until thickened. Cool, then stir in the onions. Add to the liver mixture in the processor and pulse briefly.

Transfer to a large terrine, cover with foil and a lid, then stand the terrine in a roasting pan. Half-fill the pan with water, then transfer to a preheated oven and cook at 400°F for 20 minutes. Remove the lid and foil and bake, uncovered, for a further 20 minutes. When cooked, the pâté will shrink away from the sides of the terrine. Cool and chill overnight, then serve.

I love the salty, sour flavor of these lemons. Before you use them in a recipe, take out of the brine, remove and discard the flesh, then slice the peel and use in recipes. The peel is also good with black olives.

preserved lemons
for Moroccan chicken tagine

8 lemons

¾ cup salt

6 cloves

2 cinnamon sticks

6 cardamom pods

2 fresh bay leaves

Chicken tagine

2 pinches of saffron threads

1 whole chicken

1 inch fresh ginger, finely sliced

2 garlic cloves, finely sliced

2 tablespoons olive oil

2 large onions, grated

2 cinnamon sticks

sliced peel of 1 preserved lemon

salt and freshly ground black pepper

20 black olives

Serves 4

Cut 6 of the lemons in quarters lengthwise, leaving them attached at the stem end. Cram 1 tablespoon salt into the slits of each lemon and push the fruit into a preserving jar. Add the cinnamon, cardamom, and bay leaves. Add the remaining 6 tablespoons salt to the jar, add the juice of the 2 remaining lemons, and top up with boiling water. Seal and use after 2 weeks.

To use, remove the lemon from the brine and scrape out and discard the flesh. Use the peel cut into slices with chicken tagines and other stews.

Chicken tagine with preserved lemons Soak the saffron in ¼ cup boiling water for 30 minutes. Make slits in the breast of the chicken and insert slivers of ginger and garlic. Heat the oil in a large casserole dish, add the chicken, and brown on all sides until golden. Add the onions, saffron and its soaking water, cinnamon sticks, and the preserved lemon peel. Add 1 cup water, a pinch of salt, and freshly ground black pepper. Cover with a lid, bring to a boil, and simmer on top of the stove or cook in a preheated oven at 300°F until tender. Stir in the olives and serve.

Alternatively, add the lemon and olives for the last 10 minutes of cooking (this is the traditional way).

I am a great fan of curds—they're delicious in tarts, good on toast, and hellishly decadent with croissants. I use mango purée from India to make this—but you could use fresh mango (just make sure it's superbly ripe and sweet) or frozen mango, blended to a purée.

mango and ginger curd
with croissants

1 cup mango purée

2 inches fresh ginger, peeled and grated

grated zest of 1 lime and freshly squeezed juice of ½ lime

¾ cup sugar

6 tablespoons unsalted butter, cut into cubes

4 eggs, beaten

freshly baked croissants, brioche, or toast, to serve

Makes about 3 cups

Put the mango, ginger, lime zest, lime juice, and sugar into a non-reactive (stainless steel or enamel) saucepan and heat until simmering. Simmer for about 5 minutes, then strain into a heatproof bowl. Discard the residue.

Put the bowl over a saucepan of gently simmering water and add the butter. Stir until melted.

Strain the eggs through a fine strainer into the bowl and stir well. Cook gently, stirring often at the beginning, then continuously at the end, until the mixture coats the back of a spoon, about 45 minutes. Do not let boil or the mixture will separate.

Remove from the heat and pour into warm, sterilized preserving jars (see page 59). Seal and let cool. Use immediately with croissants, or store in the refrigerator for up to 1 week.

sweet things

This sauce is based on a delicious lemon and passionfruit curd. Mix it with 3 tablespoons cream and churn into an ice cream, or dilute with lemon juice and rum to make this wonderful sauce.

passionfruit and rum sauce
with ice cream

4 large, ripe passionfruit

1 teaspoon finely grated lemon zest and the freshly squeezed juice of 1 lemon

6 tablespoons unsalted butter, cut into cubes

1¼ cups sugar

3 eggs, beaten

To serve

juice of 1 lemon

1 tablespoon sugar

2 tablespoons white rum

vanilla ice cream

Makes about 3 cups

Cut the tops off the passionfruit and scoop the pulp and seeds into a bowl.

Put the lemon zest, lemon juice, butter, and sugar into a heatproof bowl set over a saucepan of gently simmering water. Don't let the bottom of the bowl touch the water.

Heat gently, stirring, until the sugar dissolves and the butter melts.

Strain the eggs through a fine strainer into the bowl and stir well. Cook gently, stirring often at the beginning, then continuously at the end, until the mixture coats the back of a spoon, about 30–40 minutes. Do not let boil or the mixture will separate.

Remove from the heat and stir in the passionfruit pulp. Pour into warm sterilized jars.* Seal and let cool. Use immediately or store in the refrigerator for up to 1 week.

When ready to serve, mix the sugar and rum to dissolve the sugar, then stir 1 tablespoon of the mixture into the curd. Add the remaining mixture, a little at a time, until you reach a pouring consistency. Spoon the sauce over the ice cream and serve.

*Sterilizing preserving jars Wash the jars in hot, soapy water, and rinse in boiling water. Put into a large saucepan and cover with hot water. With the lid on, bring the water to a boil, and continue boiling for 15 minutes. Turn off the heat, then leave the jars in the hot water until just before they are to be filled. Invert the jars onto a clean cloth to dry. Sterilize the lids for 5 minutes, by boiling or according to the manufacturer's instructions. The jars should be filled and sealed while they are still hot. For useful guidelines, see website http://hgic.clemson.edu/factsheets/HGIC3040.htm.

Peanut butter is the easiest thing in the world to make yourself. Make it with other nuts, such as the cashews here, and it's even more interesting. The chocolate-bitter flavor contrasts nicely with the cinnamon toast. If you like your nut butter sweeter, by all means add some sugar, but try it like this first. This recipe makes a smooth butter—if you like some crunch, reserve some of the nuts, chop coarsely, then stir them in at the end.

chocolate cashew butter
with cinnamon toast

1 cup unsalted cashew nuts

a small pinch of salt

1½–3 tablespoons safflower oil

6 squares bittersweet chocolate

Cinnamon toast

8 thick slices of bread

sugar

ground cinnamon

Serves 4

To make the nut butter, put the nuts and salt into a blender and grind until smooth. With the motor running, drizzle in the oil in a thin stream until creamy. You may have to scrape down the sides of the bowl.

Put the chocolate into a bowl and microwave on HIGH for about 1 minute, or until softened. Alternatively, melt in a heatproof bowl set over a saucepan of gently simmering water. Scrape the chocolate into the nut mixture and blend again. (I like the butter more runny—add a little extra oil to achieve this.) Chill the cashew butter until ready to serve.

Cinnamon toast Put the bread under a preheated broiler and toast on one side only. Put the sugar and cinnamon into a bowl, mix evenly, then dust over the other side. Broil that side until the sugar melts and the mixture is brown. Serve with a bowl of chocolate cashew butter.

This glorious sauce comes from Denmark, where it is made with raspberries (*hindbaer*) or strawberries (*jordbaer*). My mother used it as a sauce for Danish Christmas rice pudding, a creamy rice concoction I liked much better than the ordinary baked version. In any case, use this sauce with ice cream and other creamy puddings, or add more juice and churn it into a sorbet.

red berry sauce
for waffles and ice cream

2 baskets raspberries or strawberries, about 12 oz.–1 lb.

freshly squeezed juice of ½ small lemon

⅛ cup sugar

2 teaspoons cornstarch

2 teaspoons brandy

strawberry or raspberry ice cream, or sweetened whipped cream, to serve

Crispy waffles

1½ cups all-purpose flour

¼ teaspoon salt

½ tablespoon baking powder

2 eggs, separated

1 cup milk

1 tablespoon butter, melted

Serves 4

If using raspberries, pick them over. If using strawberries, wash them, pat dry on paper towels, then hull them. Put the berries and lemon juice into a saucepan, add the sugar, and bring to a boil, stirring often. Simmer until the juice has come out of the berries, then strain through a fine strainer, pushing through as much pulp as possible. Discard the residue.

Taste the juice and add more sugar to taste. Mix the cornstarch in a bowl with 2 teaspoons water until smooth (this is called "slaking"). Reheat the juice and stir in the cornstarch. Cook, stirring constantly, until the juice is slightly thickened and clear (the cornstarch makes it clear and sparkling). Cool, then stir in the brandy. Serve with waffles topped with ice cream or whipped cream.

Crispy waffles Sift the flour, salt, and baking powder into a bowl and make a well in the center. Beat the egg yolks until creamy. Put the egg whites into a second bowl and beat until stiff and frothy. Pour the melted butter into the flour, then the egg yolks and milk. Mix well, then fold in the beaten egg whites.

Heat the waffle iron until smoking (or as recommended by the manufacturer), pour a little batter into each compartment, and spread over quickly. Cook as directed by the manufacturer, then transfer the waffle to a heated plate and cook the remaining mixture in the same way. If using a large, electric waffle iron, break the waffles into segments, then serve. The waffles can be kept in a warm oven for about 20 minutes. They can also be frozen and reheated from frozen in a preheated oven at 350°F for 10 minutes.

index

conversion charts

Weights and measures have been rounded up
or down slightly to make measuring easier.

Volume equivalents:

American	Metric	Imperial
1 teaspoon	5 ml	
1 tablespoon	15 ml	
¼ cup	60 ml	2 fl.oz.
⅓ cup	75 ml	2½ fl.oz.
½ cup	125 ml	4 fl.oz.
⅔ cup	150 ml	5 fl.oz. (¼ pint)
¾ cup	175 ml	6 fl.oz.
1 cup	250 ml	8 fl.oz.

Weight equivalents: Measurements:

Imperial	Metric	Inches	Cm
1 oz.	25 g	¼ inch	5 mm
2 oz.	50 g	½ inch	1 cm
3 oz.	75 g	¾ inch	1.5 cm
4 oz.	125 g	1 inch	2.5 cm
5 oz.	150 g	2 inches	5 cm
6 oz.	175 g	3 inches	7 cm
7 oz.	200 g	4 inches	10 cm
8 oz. (½ lb.)	250 g	5 inches	12 cm
9 oz.	275 g	6 inches	15 cm
10 oz.	300 g	7 inches	18 cm
11 oz.	325 g	8 inches	20 cm
12 oz.	375 g	9 inches	23 cm
13 oz.	400 g	10 inches	25 cm
14 oz.	425 g	11 inches	28 cm
15 oz.	475 g	12 inches	30 cm
16 oz. (1 lb.)	500 g		
2 1b.	1 kg		

Oven temperatures:

110°C	(225°F)	Gas ¼
120°C	(250°F)	Gas ½
140°C	(275°F)	Gas 1
150°C	(300°F)	Gas 2
160°C	(325°F)	Gas 3
180°C	(350°F)	Gas 4
190°C	(375°F)	Gas 5
200°C	(400°F)	Gas 6
220°C	(425°F)	Gas 7
230°C	(450°F)	Gas 8
240°C	(475°F)	Gas 9